Presidents' Day

ABDO
Publishing Company

A Buddy Book
by
Julie Murray

MID-CONTINENT PUBLIC LIBRARY

3 0001 01266492 8

Visit us at
www.abdopub.com

Published by ABDO Publishing Company, 4940 Viking Drive, Edina, Minnesota 55435.

Printed in the United States.

Edited by: Sarah Tieck
Contributing Editor: Michael P. Goecke
Graphic Design: Denise Esner
Image Research: Deborah Coldiron, Maria Hosley
Photographs: Corel, Eyewire, Hulton Archives, North Wind Archives, Photodisc

Library of Congress Cataloging-in-Publication Data

Murray, Julie, 1969-
  Presidents' Day / Julie Murray.
      p. cm. — (Holidays)
  Includes bibliographical references (p.) and index.
  ISBN 1-59197-590-5
      1. Presidents' Day—Juvenile literature. 2. Presidents—United States—Juvenile literature.
  [1. Presidents' Day. 2. Presidents. 3. Holidays.] I. Title.

E176.8.M87 2004
394.261—dc22

                                        2003066009

Table of Contents

What Is Presidents' Day?

Presidents' Day is a **federal holiday** in the United States. It is celebrated on the third Monday in February. It celebrates all the presidents of the United States.

People used to celebrate this holiday with parties and balls. Now, banks, government offices, and schools close.

The First Presidents' Day

The first Presidents' Day was in 1796. It celebrated the first president. But, it was not called Presidents' Day then. It was known as George Washington's Birthday.

George Washington was the first president.

People were thankful for George Washington. He was the first president. He led the fight for freedom from England's rule.

The whole country celebrated George Washington's birthday on February 22, 1796. They celebrated every year after that. Soon, it became a **holiday**.

Another president's birthday was also a holiday. This was Abraham Lincoln's birthday, on February 12.

Abraham Lincoln was the 16th president.

Abraham Lincoln was president from 1861 to 1865. He led the United States through the **Civil War**. He helped free the **slaves**.

President Lincoln was shot and killed in 1865. People wanted to remember him. So, they began to celebrate his birthday every year.

In 1971, President Richard Nixon called the third Monday in February Presidents' Day. He said it would celebrate all past presidents.

President Nixon set the date for the holiday.

Other Famous Presidents

Thomas Jefferson

Thomas Jefferson was president from 1801 to 1809. He helped write the **Declaration of Independence**. He also helped the United States gain more land. This was called the Louisiana Purchase. It added a lot of the western part of the United States.

Theodore Roosevelt

Theodore Roosevelt was president from 1901 to 1909. He saved 150 million acres (607 million ha) of land for national forests. Theodore Roosevelt took office at age 42. That made him the youngest president in history.

Theodore Roosevelt was the 26th president.

Franklin D. Roosevelt was president during World War II.

Franklin D. Roosevelt

Franklin D. Roosevelt was president from 1933 to 1945. He helped the United States during the **Great Depression**. He also led the country through **World War II**.

The U.S. Presidents

1. George Washington 1789-1797
2. John Adams 1797-1801
3. Thomas Jefferson 1801-1809
4. James Madison 1809-1817
5. James Monroe 1817-1825
6. John Quincy Adams 1825-1829
7. Andrew Jackson 1829-1837
8. Martin Van Buren 1837-1841
9. William Henry Harrison 1841
10. John Tyler 1841-1845
11. James K. Polk 1845-1849
12. Zachary Taylor 1849-1850
13. Millard Fillmore 1850-1853
14. Franklin Pierce 1853-1857
15. James Buchanan 1857-1861
16. Abraham Lincoln 1861-1865
17. Andrew Johnson 1865-1869
18. Ulysses S. Grant 1869-1877
19. Rutherford B. Hayes 1877-1881
20. James A. Garfield 1881

21. Chester A. Arthur 1881-1885
22. Grover Cleveland 1885-1889
23. Benjamin Harrison 1889-1893
24. Grover Cleveland 1893-1897
25. William McKinley 1897-1901
26. Theodore Roosevelt 1901-1909
27. William H. Taft 1909-1913
28. Woodrow Wilson 1913-1921
29. Warren G. Harding 1921-1923
30. Calvin Coolidge 1923-1929
31. Herbert Hoover 1929-1933
32. Franklin D. Roosevelt 1933-1945
33. Harry S. Truman 1945-1953
34. Dwight D. Eisenhower 1953-1961
35. John F. Kennedy 1961-1963
36. Lyndon B. Johnson 1963-1969
37. Richard M. Nixon 1969-1974
38. Gerald R. Ford 1974-1977
39. Jimmy Carter 1977-1981
40. Ronald Reagan 1981-1989
41. George H. W. Bush 1989-1993
42. Bill Clinton 1993-2001
43. George W. Bush 2001-

What Is A President's Job?

The president of the United States is in charge of the country. The president helps make laws, gives speeches, and visits other countries.

The president is in charge of the federal government. The president signs in new laws, makes sure that laws are followed, and picks people for some government jobs.

The president is commander-in-chief of the army, the navy, and the air force.

The president is also in charge of the armed forces. This includes the army, the navy, the air force, and other military forces.

Who Can Be President?

The United States of America is a type of **democracy**. Democracy is a kind of government.

The **citizens** of the United States vote for the president. The person who is elected is president for four years. Each president can be elected twice.

Citizens vote to elect the president and other leaders.

Almost any person can be president of the United States. But there are three requirements:

1. Must be at least 35 years old.

2. Must be a **citizen** of the United States at birth.

3. Must have lived in the United States for at least 14 years.

Presidential Landmarks

There are many different landmarks around the United States. Some honor past presidents. Many people visit them on Presidents' Day.

Mount Rushmore

Mount Rushmore is in the Black Hills of South Dakota. Four faces are carved into the rocky cliff. The faces are of George Washington, Thomas Jefferson, Theodore Roosevelt, and Abraham Lincoln.

The carving of Mount Rushmore was completed on October 31, 1941.

The White House

The current president lives in the White House. It is in Washington, D.C. Washington, D.C., is the **capital** of the United States.

The White House has been home to each president since 1800.

The Washington Monument (left) and Lincoln Memorial.

Washington Monument and Lincoln Memorial

The Washington Monument and Lincoln Memorial are in Washington, D.C. One honors George Washington. The other honors Abraham Lincoln.

Mount Vernon

George Washington's home was Mount Vernon. It is in Virginia. The house where George Washington once lived is still there. So is his grave.

Visitors can tour George Washington's home.

Important Words

capital a city where government leaders meet.

citizen a member of a state or nation.

Civil War the United States war from 1861 to 1865. People in the North fought against people in the South.

Declaration of Independence a very important paper from 1776 that explained America was ready to rule itself.

democracy a type of government in which citizens rule themselves.

federal holiday a government holiday in the United States.

Great Depression the time between 1930 and 1940 when the world's economy was struggling.

holiday a special time for celebration.

slave a person who can be bought and sold.

World War II a war fought in Europe and Asia. America was involved from 1941 to 1945.

Web Sites

To learn more about Presidents' Day,

visit ABDO Publishing Company on the World Wide Web. Web site links about Presidents' Day are featured on our Book Links page. These links are routinely monitored and updated to provide the most current information available.

www.abdopub.com

Index